C000006407

1 MONTH OF
FREE
READING

at

www.ForgottenBooks.com

By purchasing this book you are
eligible for one month membership to
ForgottenBooks.com, giving you
unlimited access to our entire
collection of over 1,000,000 titles via
our web site and mobile apps.

To claim your free month visit:

www.forgottenbooks.com/free948593

* Offer is valid for 45 days from date of purchase. Terms and conditions apply.

ISBN 978-0-260-44528-5
PIBN 10948593

This book is a reproduction of an important historical work. Forgotten Books uses
state-of-the-art technology to digitally reconstruct the work, preserving the original format
whilst repairing imperfections present in the aged copy. In rare cases, an imperfection in
the original, such as a blemish or missing page, may be replicated in our edition. We do,
however, repair the vast majority of imperfections successfully; any imperfections that
remain are intentionally left to preserve the state of such historical works.

Forgotten Books is a registered trademark of FB &c Ltd.
Copyright © 2018 FB &c Ltd.
FB &c Ltd, Dalton House, 60 Windsor Avenue, London, SW19 2RR.
Company number 08720141. Registered in England and Wales.

For support please visit www.forgottenbooks.com

The

STUDENTS' HANDBOOK

of

STATE TEACHERS COLLEGE

INDIANA, PA.

1937-1938   Vol. X

Published by

The'

STUDENT COUNCIL

TABLE OF CONTENTS

GETTING ACQUAINTED

DR. SAMUEL FAUSOLD

GREETINGS

The Class of 1941 enters this college at a most auspicious moment. The times are challenging not only to the professional staff but to students as well. Each freshman will find a number of immediate problems facing him. He must decide upon departments and courses which will be most helpful to him and must make choices as to contacts with students and teachers. These contacts are a vital part of the college life. He must begin at once the development of professional attitudes. If he finds this to be a laborious task, he should frankly choose another profession and drop out of the 'institution. Only capable students and those sincerely interested in teaching should spend time, money, and effort in a state teachers college. It is my conviction that most members of the class now entering Indiana will successfully meet this criterion and will remain to be graduated four years hence.

The whole environment here is largely what the students make it. They will immediately begin to contribute to this environment. I am hopeful that their contribution will be constructive, not only keeping the institution on a high plane, but creating for it even a higher one.

I extend best wishes and heartiest greetings to each member of the Class of 1941.

Dr. Samuel Fausold.

COLLEGE CALENDAR
First Semester 1937 - 1938

Final Date for Entrance
Examinations—Tuesday, Sept. 7

Registration and Classification of
Freshmen—Wednesday, Sept. 8

Registration Day—All Others
Thursday, Sept. 9

Classes Begin   Friday, Sept. 10

Thanksgiving Recess Begins—12 M.
Wednesday, Nov. 24

Thanksgiving Recess Ends—12 M.
Monday, Nov. 29

Christmas Recess Begins—after
last class—Wednesday, Dec. 22

Christmas Recess Ends—12 M.
Tuesday, January 4

First Semester Ends
Friday, January 14

Second Semester 1937 - 1938

Second Semester Begins—12 M.
Tuesday, January 18

Easter Recess Begins—after last
class—Thursday, April 14

Easter Recess Ends—12 M.
Monday, April 25

Class Work Ends—after last class
Friday, May 20

Alumni Day   Saturday, May 21

Baccalaureate Service
Sunday, May 22

Senior Day   Monday, May 23

Commencement   Tuesday, May 24

TO THE WOMEN

"See first that the design is wise and just: that ascertained, pursue it resolutely."

The State Teachers College at Indiana, Pennsylvania, for more than half a century has sent women from its halls, women of sterling qualities, refinement and culture, to hold positions of honor and trust in their respective fields of service.

Yours is the opportunity to join this professional group; by honest, earnest endeavor to develop a personality that stands for individuality, reliability, and inspiration.

May you have many happy, challenging experiences in this, your pursuit. Indiana cordially welcomes you.

Hope Stewart, Dean of Women.

GREETINGS

I wish to extend greetings to the men, and especially to the Freshmen of the Indiana State Teachers College. You are welcome to the campus, to a share in its pleasures and to the great opportunity it affords you for intellectual training and self-development. College represents opportunity. Getting and giving an education is a cooperative affair.

Indiana wants to help you realize every worthy ambition and it will gladly do its full share toward that end.

W. M. Whitmyre, Dean of Men.

HISTORY OF THE SCHOOL

With the tradition of the more than fifty years of its existence behind it, Indiana now ranks in age and size with the first of Pennsylvania's Teachers Colleges.

In May, 1875, when the school was formally opened, under the direction of Dr. E. B. Fairfield, the physical property of the school consisted solely of John Sutton Hall. During the succeeding quarter century, Clark Hall, a dormitory for men, and Wilson Hall, a teacher training center, were built.

While Indiana was still a normal school, Leonard Hall, a class room and laboratory building, and a modern power plant were built, and alterations were made in Sutton Hall.

Indiana became a State Teachers College in the Spring of 1927, with the power to grant degrees in five different fields. An increased enrollment and a steadily broadening curriculum made a new Gymnasium and new Arts Building necessary.

The Gymnasium has made possible a better physical training and a wider range of physical activities for the students of Indiana. The equipment of the Arts Building, housing the Departments of Commerce, Art, and Home Economics, has helped these departments to establish themselves as leaders in their lines of education.

In the last few years other improvements have been made in the school plant; new and well-equipped science laboratories have been built in Lonard Hall; an annex has been built o West Parlor; the College green house has been enlarged; more tennis courts have been built on East Campus. The College Lodge situated on a college-owned farm just outside of the city, is a gathering place for students and faculty members at all seasons of the year.

During the last summer a new shop building was constructed near the power house. This has made it possible to remove all the shops from the basement of Sutton Hall and the space thus vacated can be used for other purposes. The new building program promises great things for the future of Indiana not only in the way of material equipment but in the posibilities of greater service.

STUDENT GOVERNMENT

STUDENT CO-OPERATIVE ASSOCIATION

This Association, organized in the Fall of 1933, is the one that every student joins. This organization makes possible our College Bookroom; the Year Book; the Indiana Penn; our lectures and entertainment; our varsity and intramural athletic activities for men and women; and many other activities of equal value.

Its policy and management is directed by a Treasurer-Manager, fifteen members of the Student Council, and seven members of the faculty appointed by the President.

This organization is vitally concerned with promoting many of the important phases of the College Student Welfare Program.

STUDENT COUNCIL OF THE STATE TEACHERS COLLEGE INDIANA, PENNSYLVANIA

Article I—Name

The name of this organization shall be the Student Council of the State Teachers College, Indiana, Pennsylvania.

Article II—Purpose

The purpose of this organization shall be:

1.   To promote in every way possible the best interest of the State Teachers College, Indiana, Pennsylvania.

2.   To regulate all matters of student conduct which do not fall under the jurisdiction of the faculty, together with such other business as may be referred to it by the President of the College, or the Faculty Committee composed of the Dean of Women, Dean of Men, and Dean of Instruction. All suggestions from students should first be presented to the Student Council.

3.   To provide a more perfect organization which will maintain the ideals of the College by student co-operation.

4.   To promote the scholastic and moral tone of the College and thus

to maintain high standards of honor, loyalty and service.

5. To constitute a medium for the expression of initiative and the exercise of judgment in the management of student affairs.

6. To aid in the maintenance of good order in the college community.

Article III—Membership

The membership of this Council shall be as follows:

1. Four representatives from the Senior Class, one of whom shall be a woman day student.

2. Four representatives from the Junior Class.

3. Three representatives from the Sophomore Class.

4. Two representatives from the Freshmen Class.

5. One representative from the Women's Resident Student League

6. One representative from the Men's Student League.

Article IV—Nomination and Election

Section I—Nomination

Each Class shall elect a Nominating Committee of three members, which committee shall prepare a list of nominees for the Council. This list shall be published not less than one week before the election. There shall be no floor nominations.

Section II—Election

Election of the members of the Council shall be held during a regularly called meeting of the class during the last week in April; these members shall take office the following September.

At the same meeting of the Junior Class at which a nominating Committee is elected, one of the Junior members of the student Council shall be elected as a Senior representative for the following year.

Article V—Term of Office
The term of office shall begin the first day of school in September of each year, and continue until the close of the second semester.

Article VI—Qualifications
Each member must be a reguluariy enrolled student, carrying not less than 16 hours of work with at least a 'C' average, and remaining in good standing.

Article VII—Vacancies
All vacancies shall be filled by a special election, except when six weeks unexpired term is left, in which case the remaining members of the Council shall elect a member for the unexpired term.

Article VIII—Officers
The officers of the Student Council shall be President, Vice-President and Secretary-Treasurer.

The officers shall be selected by the Council from its own membership, but the President must be a Degree Senior.

Article IX—Powers and Duties
1. It shall be the duty of the Council to consider such matters of student interest as may be presented by the students, either through recognized organizations or individually. The Council may also consider such matters of student importance

as appear to offer an opportunity for helpful suggestions.

2. It shall be the duty of the Council to consider from the student viewpoint, such matters as may be referred to it by the President of the College or by the Faculty Committee.

3. It shall be the duty of the Council to make suggestions and recommendations to the Faculty Committee concerning matters that have been considered.

4. It shall be the duty of the Council to deal with student problems and to make recommendations concerning matters of importance or interest.

5. Any action taken by the Council relating to legislation, administration, and disciplinary problems involving student relationships to the institution shall be subject to the veto powers of the President of the Institution.

Article X—Meetings

Regular meetings shall be held at least once per month during the school year. Other meetings may be called by the President of the Council or by the Faculty Committee.

The Council may meet in joint session with the Faculty Committee whenever there are recommendations for consideration.

Article XI—Quorum

Ten members shall constitute a quorum.

THE MEN'S STUDENT LEAGUE

Article 1—Name

The name of this organization shall be "The Men's Student League of the State Teachers College Indiania, Pennsylvania."

Article II—Purpose

The purpose of this organization shall be to cooperate with the administrative authorities of the college for the promotion of personal and group responsibility in the guidance and regulation of the affairs of all men students.

Article III—Membership

Members in this league shall consist of all men students registered in the college.

Article IV—Officers

1. The Executive Board of the league shall be composed of two representatives from each of the Senior, Junior, Sophomore and Freshmen classes.

2. The members of the Executive Board must each be a regularly enrolled student carrying not less than sixteen hours of work with at least a "C" average, and in good standing.

3. The Executive Board shall be elected at a meeting of the men students called during the first four weeks of the school year.

4. The term of office shall begin the first week of October of each year, and continue until the close of the second semester.

5. The Executive Board shall choose its own President.

6. The quorum requirement shall be six members.

7. The members of the Executive Board may choose another representative from the same class in case of a vacancy.

8. The Dean of Men shall be an ex-officio member of the Executive Board.

9. The President of the Executive Board shall be the Men's Student League representative to the Student Council.

Article V—Meetings

1. The League shall consider and act upon such matters as may be brought before it by the Dean of Men, or any other male student.

2. Meetings may be called by the officers of the league or by the Dean of Men.

Article VI—Powers and Duties

1. The function of the League is to deal with the problems of men students in a way which is consistent with the policies of responsible authority.

2. The league is authorized to make complete list of Freshmen customs.

3. The League is authorized to appoint five members of the Sophomore class who will act as a tribunal in the enforcement of the Freshmen customs.

RESIDENT WOMEN'S STUDENT LEAGUE

Article I—Name

The name of this organization shall be "The Resident Women's Student League of the State Teachers College, Indiana, Pennsylvania."

Article II—Objectives

1. The regulation of conditions for the promotion of happiness, good health and right living.

2. The promotion of conditions for the development of courtesy, self-control, cooperation, high ethical standards, and thoroughly professioual attitude toward work.

3. The development of individual and group responsibility.

4. The stimulation of good fellowship and the recognition of lawful authority.

Article III—Membership

The Women Students of Indiana State Teachers College are in a large manner self-governing in spirit, but for practical purposes all women students under dormitory regulations are divided into unit groups, approximately respectively thirty-five to fifty students. These various groups make plans for their guidance in regard to conduct. Each member is personally responsible for upholding the regulations of the League. Membership in this League shall consist of all women students registered in the college who live in the school dormitories or cottages under dormitory regulations.

The unit groups elect their own officers such as Light Proctors, Fire Proctors. These proctors serve more as friendly advisers to their groups. A representative is chosen from each group unit. Eligibility to this office depends upon scholarship and conduct. A faculty member sponsors every unit group.

Article IV—Officers

The Executive Board of the League shall be composed of the Dean of Women and one representative in each corridor group in John Sutton Hall, three representatives from Clark Hall, and representation from cottages according to group location. The members of the Executive Board whenever possible shall be chosen from those who have been residents of the halls at least one year. The officers shall be chosen at the first meeting.

Article V—Meetings Corridor Group

A regular meeting shall be held by each corridor group once a month. the time to be decided upon by the Executive Board.

1. Each representative shall call and preside at the meeting of her group. Whenever possible the Faculty Sponsor shall be present at the meeting.

2. Each representative shall be in close co-operation with the Proctors in her group and shall hold regular meetings for the purpose of hearing reports and making suggestions for the guidance of the group.

3. Each corridor group shall elect proctors after consultation with the Faculty Sponsor.

4. Each Proctor shall perform the corridor duties as assigned.

THE EXECUTIVE BOARD

A regular monthly meeting shall be held.

1. This board shall have full power to see that the regulations of the Resident Women's Student League are kept.

2. Any student thought to be guilty of violating any regulations of the League shall be reported to the representative of said group.

3. The group in which any offense is said to occur shall, when necessary, state the case to the Executive Board.

4. Repeated offenses reported to the Executive Board shall be kept in the files of the Women's Student League.

5. Special committees shall be appointed.

BY-LAWS
Article 1—Officers and Committees of Resident Women's Student League

It shall be the duty of the President:

1. To preside at the meetings.

2. To call meetings when necessary.

3. To be ipso-facto member of each corridor group.

VICE PRESIDENT

The Vice President shall be the Chief Executive in the temporary absence of the President.

SECRETARY

The Secretary shall keep the minutes of the meetings of the League, carry on all correspondence, post notices for meetings, and keep lists of all officers and committees.

THE DEAN OF WOMEN

The Dean of Women shall be ex-officio member of the Executive Board.

SOCIAL COMMITTEE

There shall be a committee composed of five members.

Article II—Election of Officers

The officers of the Resident Women's Student League shall be elected the first meeting in October.

The officers shall hold office until the close of the second semester. Any vacancies shall be filled by the Executive Board.

RULES FOR FRESHMEN MEN

1. Freshmen men must begin customs on the day dinks are offered for sale.

2. Freshmen must wear dinks, black four-in-hand ties, and black

socks.   The dinks are standardized and are the colors of the school.

3.   Freshmen shall keep coats or sweaters completely buttoned when in public.

4.   Freshmen must not use tobacco in any form when in public.

5.   Freshmen must not loiter around Clark Hall.

6.   Every Freshman shall wear, during the first one week of college, a card upon which is legibly printed his name in large black letters not less than one inch high.

7.   There shall be no dating on or off the campus.

8.   Freshmen must attend all assemblies and Vesper services.

9.   Freshmen must attend all athletic contests.

10.   Freshmen shall learn Victory Song and Alma Mater.

11.   Freshmen shall always be neatly dressed and have shoes shined.

12.   There shall be no hazing.

13.   No upper-classmen has the right to excuse any freshman from customs.

14.   Customs shall continue for one month.

15.   Freshmen may dance Monday, Wednesday and Saturday nights.

16.   .The Sophomore Tribunal consists of five men appointed by the Men's League.   This Tribunal is a Sophomore organization only and shall see that Freshmen customs are enforced.

DORMITORY REGULATIONS

Study hour is observed from 7:15 until 9:45 P. M. You will soon find this time is all too short; make the most of it while it lasts. There is plenty of time during the day and on Saturday evening for social visits.

Each hall and cottage has a resident faculty member. You will soon meet her at a hall meeting. Consider her a friend and advisor.

A room is provided in the basement of John Sutton Hall equipped with modern electrical equipment, including a drier and numerous irons for washing and pressing clothes. All laundry must be done in this room which is open all day. Adjoining the laundry is an up-to-date shampoo room equipped with lavatories and electrical driers for washing and drying hair. There is adequate mirror space and light for setting hair.

Indiana is very fortunate in having three elevators in John Sutton Hall. An admirable courtesy of stepping aside for guests of the school and faculty has become established. Because of the great number of students living on the third and fourth floors, students living on second floors are not expected to use the elevators.

WOMEN DAY STUDENTS

Rooms on the first floor north corridor of John Sutton Hall have been reserved for women day students. Convenient arrangements have been made in these different rooms for study, lunching, and lounging in addition to the rest rooms for women in the gymnasium.

It is the wish of the college to give day students opportunity for pleasant social contacts and activities as they desire. This past year, social dancing at noon offered diversion and practice for a considerable number of students, and an outing at the school lodge and an afternoon party in Recreation Hall were other features of the year's activities. This program can be extended to meet the needs and wishes of the group.

DINING ROOM

Regular tables will be assigned as soon as possible. Faculty and upper classmen occupy the heads of the tables. These places should be left vacant unless otherwise directed by persons in charge of the dining room.

No service is begun until after the Grace bell has rung.

Breakfast is served from 7:00 until 7:30 A. M. Students may enter the dining room any time before 7:30. Lunch is served at 12:20 every day except Saturday when it is served at 12:00. Dinner is served at 6:00 every day except Sunday. Breakfast is served from 8:00 until 8:30 on Sundays. Dinner is at 1:00 and tea at 5:45 Sunday.

STUDENT HEALTH

The health of the students is usually very good, but if ill at any time report to the Infirmary. Do not endanger the health of others by remaining in your room when ill.

Illness must be reported, either by yourself, your roommate, or friend before classes convene if you wish to be excused. Absence from classes because of illness is excused only by the nurses in charge of the infirmary. Infirmary hours, except in case of emergency, are adhered to as follows:

7:30 to 10:30 A. M.
1:00 to 2:00 P. M.
4:00 to 5:00 P. M.
7:00 to 8:00 P. M.

Visiting hours are 4:00 to 5:00 P. M. daily except Sunday. Sunday hours are 9:30 to 10:30 A. M.

LIBRARIES

The college library is located on the first floor of John Sutton Hall and is open to all students of the college. The collection includes books and magazines for leisure as well as professional and reference reading. Students are admitted to the stacks. Books and magazines borrowed for use in or out of the library are charged at the circulation desk. Books from the "reserved books" section are read in the library during hours of opening, but may be borowed for home use at 8:30 P. M. during the week or at 11:40 A. M. on Saturday. They are returned before 8:00 A. M. on the following college morning.

Library hours:

Monday - Friday—7:45 A. M. to 5:30 P. M. and 7:00 P. M. to 9:00 P. M.

Saturday—7:45 A. M. to 2:30 P. M.

ASSEMBLIES

General assemblies are held for lectures and other entertainments and on the class of the President. Each department has its own group meetings and the many student organizations arrange their own time for regular or special assemblies.

VESPER SERVICE

The Vesper Services offer an opportunity for the students to gather together for a period of non-sectarian religious worship.

The services are conducted each Sunday evening by different campus groups. Religious questions are discussed from the viewpoints of the different groups.

These services have become an integral part of the religious life of every student at Indiana Teachers College..

DAILY BULLETIN

The Daily Bulletin is read each morning in the first classes of the day. Each student should note carefully the items of the bulletin. Important announcements are frequently made through this medium. Those desiring to make announcements through the Daily Bulletin should place them in the hands of Miss Elizabeth Treater in the President's Office before four o'clock on the day preceding the date when they are to be made public.

CO-OPERATIVE BOOK ROOM

The Co-operative Book Room is located on the main corridor of Sutton Hall. It is open from 8:00 A. M. until 5:00 P. M. to serve all students of the College. The Book Room carries a complete list of all studuents needs.

STUDENT AIDS

Indiana is fortunate in having a loan fund available for the use of advanced students. This fund was started in a small way about fifteen years ago and later taken up by the faculty and increased by entertainments and faculty and student contributions. Many contributions made by alumni to the proposed Jane E. Leonard Memorial Library were turned over to the loan fund which was then named the Jane E. Leonard Students Loan Fund. During the last few years many alumni units have made contributions and student classes and other organizations have continued to subscribe until the fund now amounts to over fifteen thousand dollars and it is hoped that the fund may be brought up to twenty-five thousand within a short time. The money is loaned to seniors who have shown ability and character in their work here. During the last year a few loans have been made to juniors but the needs of fourth-year students are cared for first.

The Y. W. C. A. has been giving a loan of fifty dollars each year to a senior girl who best meets the standards set up which includes scholarship, leadership, and active participation in the Y. W. C. A.

The College Club of Indiana, the local chapter of the D. A. R. and the local P. E. O. group have rendered some aid to worthy students.

LECTURES

One of the many activities sponsored by the Student Cooperative Association is a serious of Lectures and Entertainments The talent presented could not be purchased in large cities for the entire amount of the student fee. Recently the speeches of Will Durant, Senator Nye, and Morris Fishbein have thrilled the student body.

Excellent talent in the dramatic

and musical fields is presented. The Hedgerow Players will give a performance of Twelfth Night in November 1937. Several choral groups will visit Indiana also. Speakers engaged months ahead include Victor Heiser, author of "An American Doctor's Odyssey;" F. J. Schlink of Consumers Research; Gordon B. Enders, adviser to the Grand Lama of Tibet; and Norman Thomas, a political advocate. These are merely samples of the engaging events the Lecture Course Committee of the Student Cooperative Association will bring to you during your sojourn at Indiana.

PUBLICATIONS

STUDENT HANDBOOK

The Handbook, which is edited and published by the Student Council, is the official informer of new students at Indiana. In it are found descriptions and comments concerning all the activities of the Campus. Read it through and orient yourself with your new environment.

THE OAK

The Oak, the title of the annual publication, represents the college and its tall stately oak trees. The art motif of the 1937 Oak was a symbolic representation of the college and The Oak and made use of Bassani engravings made from original charcoal drawings. Executive positions are filled by persons elected by a committee on publications. Since the annual is an all-college publication, staff positions in the editorial, art, and business departmen' are open to all students of the college who have had experience in journalism or who have the interest and desire to gain a knowledge of yearbook planning. Applications stating experience and qualifications should be made to the Editor-in-Chief in writing before October 1, 1937.

THE INDIANA PENN

The Indiana Penn, published weekly by a regular staff made up of students deeply interested in furthering journalism, is the newspaper of the college. Each week copies of the paper are placed at convenient places in the various campus buildings. There is no charge for the newspaper because of the fact that your activity fee assessment entitles you to receive the publication which is financed by appropriations from the Student Cooperative Association's treasury.

In addition to the paper's conforming to an accepted association's standards of journalism the Penn staff tries: to justly publicize worthy student and faculty achievements; to foster interest in all the activities of the college; to inform students, parents, alumni and friends on the institution's accomplishments; to act as a unifying force for all organizations and extra-curricular activities; to promote the general welfare of the college; to advertise the college abroad.

The delivery of a finished product weekly is truly a challenge to any aggressive student's constructive ability, his ingenuity, and his ability to organize and administer the work involved in placing before the college a newsy and accurate account of the business of the school.
Editor-in-Chief .. Charles B. Wonder

TEACHERS COLLEGE BULLETIN

The Teachers College Bulletin is published four times a year. It is issued twice as college catalogue and twice as an educational bulletin.

EXPLANATION OF GRADES

"A" indicates an excellent grade of work.

"B" indicates a good grade of work.

"C" indicates a satisfactory grade of work.

"D" indicates a low grade of passing work.

"F" indicates a failure and no credit shall be given for the course so marked until it has been repeated in the regular way.

"I" is given to students who because of illness or other entirely satisfactory reasons have been unable to complete the required work, but have been doing in general a satisfactory type of work. This mark must be removed within one month after the opening of the next semester that the student is in school or become a failure. Upon completing the required amount of work the student may receive any mark to which the teacher feels he is entitled.

A system of quality points has been established as follows:

1. There are required for graduation or for permission to do student teaching a number of quality points equal to the number of semester hours credit required in the course being pursued.

2. A grade of "A" gives three quality points for each semester hour of credit so marked; a grade of "B" gives two quality points for each semester hour of credit so marked; a grade of "C" gives one quality point for each semester hour of credit so marked; and a grade of "D" gives no quality point.

ORGANIZATION AND ACTIVITIES

ALL SCHOOL ORGANIZATIONS
Y. W. C. A.

The day will bring some lovely thing,
I say it over each new dawn;
"Some gay, adventurous thing to hold
Against my heart, when it is gone."
And so I rise and go to meet
The day with wings upon my feet.

—Grace Noll Crowell

In this same spirit of adventure you can anticipate good fellowship, happy pleasures, and fine intellectual stimulation by becoming one of this great unity, the Young Women's Christian Association. The purpose of the organization is fourfold: to provide for the members opportunity for growth physically, mentally, socially, and spiritually, as was exemplified by the Great Teacher, Jesus. Since the founding of the organization on this campus forty years ago, the Y. W. C. A. has shown progress in outlook and achievement.

Beginning with the Big and Little Sister activities, climaxed by the party the first Saturday night at school, the activities of the Y. W. C. A. continue in varied program throughout the year. Meetings are held approximately every two weeks with Friday afternoon Teas occuring on the alternating weeks. The programs for the year 1937-1938, based on the theme: "What Men Live By," will present something of the religious and philosophies of life followed by people of different nationalities, with special emphasis on the religion and philosophy of life followed by college students. An opportunity for personal spiritual growth and inspiration is offered by the Morning Watch Services held in the "Y" room every Monday morning at 6:45. These fifteen minutes of meditation have proved helpful in the hurried lives of many of the women students.

The persons selected to guide the work for the following year are:

President .... Mary Stepanchak
Vice President .... Sara Stewart
Secretary .... Jane Hetrick
Treasurer .... Helen Maher
Program Chairman Alice Ellenberger
Social Chairman .... Helen Mauver
Finance Chairman ... Mary Markell
Publicity Chairman .. Phoebe Albert
Publications Chairman
                    Kathleen Simpson
Morning Watch Chairman
                    Jane Hollenbach
Music Chairman ..... Eleanor Hess
Social Service Chairman
                    Margaret Barnett

These people work with the faculty sponsors and the members of their committees in organizing and managing their work. The value of Y. W. C. A. is not measured by the work of these few alone, but by what the other 600 members contribute through active participation. All committees of the Y. W. C. A. are open to any members who wish to join them.

The Y. W. C. A. as your friend, extends to you new women students a hearty welcome,

Y. M. C. A.

The Y. M. C. A. is the one organization on the campus where all men meet in a spirit of brotherhood with the definite purpose of fostering a religious life acceptable to all creeds. Regular meetings are held each Wednesday evening at 7:15 in the "Y" room. Here are discussed topics dealing with campus life and personal religion. The discussions are informal so that students and faculty may express themselves with freedom. A few addresses by people outside of the organization complete this part of the program. In addition, the "Y" sponsors four vesper services during the year. The social life includes a party for the freshmen. Faculty Firesides, and other functions that are decided upon by the members. Every college man owes it to himself and the school to participate in this organization which provides opportunity for the growth of the whole individual.

Officers for the year 1937-1938:
President .... Clarence Chapman
Vice President ..... John Snodgrass
Secretary .... John Paulisic
Treasurer .... Perry Lewis

NEWMAN CLUB

The Newman Club, an organization of Catholic students seeks to encourage its members in their spiritual exercises and to promote cooperation with all character-developing activities of the college.

The monthly Sunday and Wednesday meetings will be continued. This year, a number of small study groups will be organized by those who are interested. The socially minded will look forward to the usual dinner, picnics and parties, which are intended to extend acquaintanceships among the members.

LEONARD LITERARY SOCIETY

The Leonard Literary Society is rich in tradition. It is the oldest and largest student organization on the campus. The Society is named for Miss Jane E. Leonard, who, for forty-nine years, was preceptress and English teacher at Indiana. Miss Leonard was one of the charter members of the literary organization.

Membership exceeds 1000. Amateur dramatic programs are presented every Monday night. Three or four professional entertainers are presented every year.

Names which appear in the professional roster of the Leonard Literary Society are: Alfred Noyes, Ruth Draper, Tong Sarg's Marionettes, the world famous Abby Players from Dublin, Ireland, Rear-Admiral Richard E. Byrd, Edythe Wynn Mathison and Charles Rann Kennedy, who are among America's greatest stage artists, Upton Close, interpreter of Asia, Carola Goya, famous Spanish dancer George Russell Irish poet, better known as A. E., Cornelia Otis Skinner, E. A. Southern, Ameri-

ca's greatest Shakespearian actor,
Ruth St. Denis, Dorothy Sands, William Bebe, Carl Sandberg, Ted Shawn
and his ensemble of men dancers,
the Miriam Winslow Dancers, Hugh
Walpole, and Christopher Morley.

Mrs. Martin Johnson, African explorer, the Jitney Players, and other
worthy talent will be presented this
season.

Each spring there is a three-act
play which represents the best technical skill and artistic finish the
students themselves can present
Among these have been: "Death
Takes a Holiday," "Journey's End,"
"Sun-Up," "Outward Bound," and
"Flowers of the Forest."

Officers for the year 1937-1938 are
as follows:

President .... Warren Davis
Vice President   Virginia Sutherland
Financial Secretary James Startzell
Secretary .... Jean Moore
Treasurer .... Betty Kanable
Adivsor .... Edna Lee Sprowls

THE TRAVELERS CLUB

The Travelers Club was organized
in October, 1927, to meet the demand
for a general travel organization to
which any student from any department and any faculty member is
eligible. Thus students and faculty
are given opportunities to share a
common interest.

The monthly meetings, held on the
first Tuesday, are vitalized by pic-

tures, exhibits, songs, games, dances and accounts of personal experiences. There is also a special social affair each semester. The programs are conducted by members of the club as well as visiting travelers and geographers. During these past years Dr. J. Russell Smith of Columbia University, an internationally known geographer, Mrs. Kathryne Whittemore of Buffalo, the Reverend James Brady of Indiana Pa., and other world travelers from far and near have appeared as speakers.

Officers for the year 1937-1938 are:
President .... Joe Sutila
Vice President .... Bill Butara
Secretary .... Martha Jane
Treasurer .... Mike Motly

EDWIN ARLINGTON ROBINSON POETRY CLUB

Organized in 1927 as the first smaller extra - curricular activity on the campus. The Robinson Poetry Club aims to promote a broader appreciation and deeper understanding of poetry by its carefully planned monthly meetings.

The club, sponsored by Miss Ruth Knowles, discusses the works of various poets in these informal programs; in the past year selections from William Butler Yeats, James Stevens, Edwin Arlington Robinson, Robert Frost and Robert Caffin were presented. However the scope of the organization is not limited to poetry alone but includes other forms of literature also.

Many of the latest books have been added to the well-chosen library, which is at the disposal of the members.

Membership is not limited to any special surriculum or to those who write poetry. Talent for writing, nevertheless, is encouraged.

THE INTERNATIONAL RELA-TIONS CLUB

The International Relations Club, which Indiana has come to know as the I. R. C., is established in the colleges and universities of the world and purposes to "fix the attention of students on those underlying principles of international conduct, interational law, and of international organization which must be agreed upon and applied if peaceful civilization is to continue." The Club operates under the Carnegie Foundation for International Peace.

The unit on the campus was formerly known as the Open Forum and upon being accepted by the International Relations Clubs, became a part of the Club's activities. The unit at Indiana is one of more than five hundred located in the United States, twenty-one of which are in Pennsylvania. There are one hundred and thirty-five Clubs in foreign countries. The Clubs in the United States are divided up into regional divisions with the Indiana unit being located in the Middle Atlantic States Division.

Membership is by invitation. Candidates are examined on the basis of scholarship with the requirement that the student must have at least a "B" average in social studies and not less than a "C" average in the other courses of study. Moreover, candidates must demonstrate an interest in national and international affairs, combined with a willingness to give time to the discussion and study of relevant material. Each unit is provided with the latest books on the subjects of international importance. These books, which are given free to the Club by the Carnegie Foundation, are located on a special shelf in the college library for the use of the club members.

THE OPEN FORUM

The Open Forum, an all-campus activity, is sponsored by the International Relations Club. The president of the International Relations Club is also Director of the Forum, while the officers of the Club act as his assistants in arranging programs.

The Forum was organized in the fall of 1933 to meet the need of organized discussion and student participation on questions of national and international importance.

Much interest and student cooperation has been manifested throughout the Forum's first years, thus placing it as one of the permanent activities of the Indiana campus.

Discussions are held bi-monthly and are led by student speakers chosen from the membership of the International Relations Club.

LIFE SAVING CLUB

The Life Saving service of the American Red Cross is a vital factor in water safety. The College Life Saving Club is a unit of this organization. The club, consisting of Senior Life Savers and Examiners of the American Red Cross, encourages good and safe swimming. Believing that correct practice tends toward perfection, this organization provides for its members opportunities for instruction and drill. Knowing that fellowship and socialization binds any group of workers, it has delightful meetings when the group has interesting programs, informal swimming, and refreshments. The big event of the year is the spring pageant and demonstration given to educate the public to this work.

DE MOLAY CLUB

The De Molay Club, one of the most recently organized clubs on the campus, was instituted Tuesday, October 17, 1933.

It is composed of present and former members of the National Order of De Molay, and is sponsored by the Masonic members of the faculty under the direction of Mr. C. M. Johnson and Mr. Risheberger. All De Molays and Master Masons, in good standing, are entitled to membership in the organization.

The purpose of the organization is to foster scholarship, fellowship, and principles of De Molay.

The organization's activities during the past year included a hamburger fry held at the school lodge, a reception given in honor of the new college president, Dr. Samuel Fausold, and the annual Spring Prom and banquet held at Rustic Lodge at which Dr. Fausold was guest of honor.

THE AMERICAN COLLEGE QUILL CLUB

The American College Quill Club is a national organization established to encourage literary efforts and to promote better writing though criticism and discussion of manuscripts presented by individual members. Indiana takes pride in the fact that Ger Rune is the only chapter to be found in a teachers college. Admission is by original manuscript only, consideration being given to the character of the applicant for responsibility and sustained effort. The biennial publication of Ger Rune is "The Scroll," but the rune also contributes regularly to "The Parchment," the national literary magazine of Quill. In matters of ritual and nomenclature, old English tradition is followed as closely as possible.

WITAN

Chancellor .... Arthur Nicholson
Vice-Chancellor
            Mrs. Helen F. Egleston
Scribe .... Roberta Caldwell
Keeper of the Parchments
            Eugene Ake
Warden of the Purse .. Lois Gorton

MUSICAL ORGANIZATIONS

THE SYMPHONIC CHOIR

This organization is distinctive in membership, in the high quality and nature of the music studied, and in the finish and thrilling quality of its concert performances. Membership is confined chiefly to Juniors and Seniors of the music department but is open to a limited number of other students on a competitive basis. Application for membership should be made to Mr. Van A. Christy, Director of Music.

Included in the repertoire are all types and schools of fine choral expression, sacred and secular, a cappella and accompanied. The choir specializes in a cappela singing of many voiced arrangements, achieving perfection of tonal colors, contrasts, balances and harmonic effects comparable in the vocal field to similar effects achieved by a fine symphony orchestra in the instrumental field.

The Symphonic Choir not only appears in concert and assembly performances in Indiana but in many high schools and communities in the surrounding territory.

THE JUNIOR A CAPPELLA CHOIR

The organization of the Junior A Cappella Choir directed by Miss Mary Muldowney completes the choral set up of the Music Department. This choir is composed of all freshmen and sophomore music students and is also open to students outside the department. The purpose of the choir is fourfold: to give first and second year music students a chance to gain a knowledge of methods and materials suitable for use in the Senior High School; to give the experience of fine ensemble singing to students who may not have a chance to sing in the Symphonic Choir; to make possible the raising of standards in the Symphonic Choir to a higher competitive basis: and to give all music students the joy and experience of singing in a group of this kind under a fine director.

THE VESPER CHOIR

The Vesper Choir, a vested chorus of women's voices, furnishes the music for the services held in the auditorium every Sunday evening throughout the school year. While the membership consists chiefly of Freshmen and Sophomore girls of the music department, a limited number of women from other curricula are admitted each year upon tryouts with the director. Two of the special annual programs should be mentioned. On the Sunday preceding the Christmas holiday is sung an impressive candle light service composed of carols and anthems, while on Palm Sunday the contrasting moods of the Passion Season and the Resurrection are portrayed in music that ranges from the medieval chants to that of our own day.

MEN'S GLEE CLUB

Any student whose voice is approved by the director is eligible to the Glee Club, the only campus choral organization devoted exclusively to men. In the past four or five years it has advanced to the front rank among extra-curricular groups, due to loyal co-operation from men of all departments and their director, Miss Borge. Included in the yearly program are appearances at various assemblies and athletic functions, and independent concert, a short program for Leonard Literary Society, and a few off campus performances in local community entertainments. Anyone interested in group singing of a rather informal type is invited to join.

LYRIC CHOIR

The Lyric Choir, a musical organization for girls, draws its membership from every department in the school. The aim of the club is twofold: to furnish real pleasure to its members through the singing of the best secular music and to contribute to the musical life of the college by appearing on programs throughout the year.

ORCHESTRA

The College Orchestra, which has been enlarged to symphonic proportions in recent years, is of particular value to those interested in fine ensemble work. Besides being a training organization for students of instruments, it serves as a practical medium for the study of various types of musical composition. Its extensive repertoire includes representative works from the classic, romantic, and modern schools. The group makes several regular assembly appearances in addition to the annual concert. Like the other musical organizations, the orchestra, while composed mostly of students of the department, is open to anyone who is accepted by Mr. L. C. Stitt, director and Miss Pearl Reed, associate director.

BAND

Under the direction of Mr. L. C. Stitt the band takes a very important part in the athletic academic, and musical life of the school. Much of the enthusiasm and vigorous spirit developed at the football games can be directly attributed to the lively influence of this group. Both in ability and size, the band has grown to proportions that warrant its being considered a well organized concert group. Emphasis is placed on a high standard of concert material rather than on march repertoire of the type frequently featured by similar college units. Membership is not confined to music students alone. All students of the school who play band instruments are urged to try out for membership in this organization.

DEPARTMENT ORGANIZATIONS

THE MUSIC CLUB

Everyone who is enrolled in the music department automatically joins the Music Club, organized to give students a voice in matters which concern them particularly. The members form a nucleus for most of the college's musical units. Departmental assemblies sponsored by this club and carried out jointly by students and faculty are usually devoted to discussions of an educational character. The group holds two annual social functions: a picnic held early in the fall and the Music Dinner.

HOME ECONOMICS CLUB

The Home Economics Club, one of the oldest extra-curricular activities at Indiana, is composed of members of the Home Economics Department. Entering students who desire membership may make an application in writing to the president before the second club meeting of the year.

The purposes of the club are to provide a means of getting acquainted with all members of the department, to give the girls practice in parliamentary procedure, to develop leadership, responsibility, dependability and resourcefulness in the girls, to promote a response to welfare and to provide opportunities for participation in various kinds of social activities.

Besides the regular monthly meetings planned by the students, an outing at the Lodge, a Freshmen-Sophomore Banquet, a Christmas Party, a May Day Breakfast, and a Junior Senior Merry-go-round, the club's activities for a year.

The club is affiliated with the state and national Home Economics Associations so that the girls receive a feeling of national consciousness.

JUNIOR CHAMBER OF COMMERCE

The Junior Chamber of Commerce organized in 1925, consists of the faculty and students of the Department of Business Education.

The Club's aim is personality development rather than professional development. Service on committees gives every student experience in organizing materials and directing people. The group hopes to broaden its interests and abilities for organizing club work in high schools.

Officers are elected by a program of activities, patterned after the Federal governmental election, of district conventions, rallies, election by ballot, and formal inauguration.

The social affairs are varied—outings in the spring and fall, stunts nights, faculty programs, and a Christmas party for the children of the Willard Home.

The present officers are:

President .... Carl Norder
1st Vice President ...... Alvin Boot
2nd Vice President .. James Startzel
Corresponding Secretary
                    Geraldine Tweed
Assist. Corresponding Secretary
                       John Ringler
Recording Secretary Kenneth Nolan
Assist. Recording Secretary
                    George Anderson
Treasurer .... Mae Armstrong
Assistant Treasurer Kathryn Averill
Sergeant-at-Arms ...... John Oyler
Doorkeepers
            Theodore Link, Donald Hess

THE INTERMEDIATE CLUB

The Intermediate Club is made up of all students registered as Intermediates in the Department Classifications. Both social and professional activities are included in the program.

The members of the group are brought in closer fellowship with the other members of the club in the many informal parties which they sponsor during the year. Some of these are held in the Activities Cottage; some, at the School Lodge; some, in Leonard Hall. In the spring, fries and early morning breakfasts are main features on the Social Calendar of the Intermediate Club.

THE PRIGRIND CLUB

All persons enrolled in the primary curriculum of the State Teachers College, Indiana, Pennsylvania are automatically members of the Prigrind Club. The name itself, Prigrind, a contraction for the earlier title of Primary Group of Indiana, implies this depatmental restriction. Organized to promote social and professional relationships among the primary students, the club has functioned as a means of unifying a particular group of students with the greater whole—the college. The third Tuesday of each month has been set aside for meetings of the Prigrind Club. Some of the meetings are professional, at which times speakers from outside the department are brought before the group, or students in the department present a program of educational interest. Other meetings are purely social affairs, for the purpose of giving opportunity to establish friendships, for providing enjoyable recreation, and for establishing an active harmonious unity which grows out of knowing people. Perhaps the social function which brings the most delightful memories is the tea-dance held each spring for the freshmen students. Plan to make your college experience happy and valuable; plan to be an active, interested member in your departmental club, from that foundation your experiences and contacts may broaden as you allow yourself to participate.

The officers for the past year, 1936-1937 were:

President
      Anne Campbell, Margaret Gray
Vice President .... Mary Lloyd
Secretary .... Betty Javens
Treasurer .... Lillian Morgan
Council: Margaret Cummins, Katha-
      leen Amos, Arlene Miller, Vir-
      ginia Anderson, Betty Jane
      Keil, Marian Walls, Betty Jane
      Wilson, Pauline Wittmer.
Sponsor .... Miss Lillian I. McLean

JOHNSTOWN STUDENT TEACH-ERS CLUB

The Johnstown Student Teachers' Club was organized by those Indiana Teachers College Students doing their student teaching in that city the first semester of 1933-34. Mrs. Wilda Lea Montgomery was the sponsor.

The purpose of the club is to bring together the members professionally in an endeavor to develop profession-al interest. A different group of majors has charge of each meeting, bringing to the students' considera-tion the majors' own field. Usually the group in charge invites its critic teachers to participate in the meet-ings. The club has proved very helpful in many ways in which the student teachers might develop and aid themselves to become better teachers.

THE MATHEMATICS CLUB

The Mathematics Club is a professional organization made up of mathematics majors and any other students interested in the subject merely as an activity. At the regular monthly meetings of the group, many phases of the field of mathematics are discussed. Some of the topics that were discussed in the 1936-37 program included: a study of the lives of great mathematicians, the problems involved in organizing and conducting a mathematics club in a high school, a discussion of books and magazines which deal with mathematics, professional organizations of the teachers of mathematics, the correlation of mathematics with other school subjects, and a study of the trends of high school requirements in mathematics especially in Pennsylvania. Doctor Reeve of Columbia University, a professional mathematician, was one of the guest speakers on this year's program.

In addition to these professional meetings, the Club enjoys a social program throughout the year. Some of this year's activities were: an outing at the school lodge in the early fall, an afternoon tea in the Activities Cottage, and several periods of mathematical games which followed the regular monthly meeting.

THE SCIENCE CLUB

The Sci-Hi Club,, under the direction of Wilber Emmert, has served the Science Majors since inception in 1925, in those phases of club work which provide for exchange of scientific ideas, furtherance of scientific interests, hobby activities, science club programs, and social well-being.

Membership is open to all science majors who elect to become affiliated with the organization and who meet certain requirements by submitting a commendable paper, demonstration, or completed project. Regular monthly meetings provide the opportunities to submit these findings. Guest speakers from the college, in the town, or from out of town often bring very much worthwhile problems to the attention of the members. A number of social affairs are regular parts of the club work. Some of these make up the whole evening's program, at other times they follow as a separate part of the monthly meeting.

The club takes an active part in the Science Conference held each year, by planning the local arrangements, taking part in the program, and assisting in many ways with the physical manipulation of the meeting.

The officers for 1937-1938 are:

President .... Wayne Henderson
Vice President .... Lois Waugaman
Secretary ... . Sara Stewart
Treasurer .. (to be elected in Sept.)
Sponsor .... Wilber Emmert

BIOLOGY CLUB

The Biology Club, under the direction of Dr. Smyth, was organized in 1932, for the purpose of fostering a greater interest in Biology and an appreciation of the out of doors.

Membership is open to those who are interested in any phase of nature.

Activities include field trips, outings, hikes, and laboratory experimentations.

ART CLUB

Founded in 1925 for the purpose of stimulating and directing interest in art, this club has given art students and faculty opportunity to fraternize as well as to carry on extracurricular activities. Though it is one of the smaller clubs its size has never deterred it from worthwhile enterprises.

It has one social function each semester. At the business meetings which are held monthly some of the best talent from various parts of the country, from the faculty, and from the student body have been heard in fine arts (including music and literature) and in general culture.

The program of the past year has purposely been quite diversified. It began as usual with a picnic at the Lodge, followed by the Art Conferences for the Service Area, in which were included lectures on modern art by Ralph M. Pearson. The next group activity was a trip to the Carnegie Art Galleries in Pittsburgh to see the International Art Exhibition. Programs of the regular meetings included a style show illustrating the changes that costume may make in personality. The annual banquet was held at Rustic Lodge, during which members of the Freshmen class gave their interpretation of the opera "Carmen," and the Jean R. McElhaney medal was awarded.

Exhibitions of the year included a series of paintings by Living American Artists, lithographic drawings by Mrs. Alma Munson Gasslander, figure sketches by Miss Grace Houston, and a group of oils by Mr. Orval Kipp.

Officers—1937-1938:
President .... Norman E. Davis
Vice-President Georgia Joyce Ripple
Secretary ... Richard Clair Thomas
Treasurer Mary Madeira Kaufman

GEOGRAPHY MAJORS CLUB

All Geography Majors became members of this Club, which was organized in 1932 to provide opportunities for participation in discussions dealing with geographic education. and to encourage personal contacts.

Conferences on geographic education were conducted in October 1935 and in March 1936 under the auspices of this Club. Geography at all school levels—primary, intermediate. secondary and college was discussed. In October, 1935, more than two hundred educators from seventy-eight different school districts became acquainted with the work of the Geography Department.   Dr. J. Russell Smith of Columbia University and other nationally and internationally known persons participated at the professional meetings of the Club.

The famous Steak Fry is a traditional activity every fall as is the Outing in the Spring, for the Club's activities are both social and professional.

SOCIAL SCIENCE CLUB

The Social Science Club was organized in 1929 for the benefit of the Social Science Majors.   All majors in this field are eligible for membership.   The purposes of the club are to provide a wider knowledge and appreciation of the field, and to encourage personal contact with the faculty.   Besides the professional meetings there are also several social gatherings during the school year. Miss Belden and Mr. Whitmyre sponsor the club.

ENGLISH ROUND TABLE

The Round Table, the professional club of the English Department, sponsored by Miss Bernice Orndorff, was organized chiefly to serve both the social and professional needs of English Majors.   The group's interest in journalism, choral reading, and dramatics, both from the standpoint of individual development and future leadership is aroused by experiencing these activities.

The English Tea in the Spring, and

the outdoor picnic in the fall, are the major social events of the club. Several professional meetings held during the year, are devoted to problems in the teaching of English, discussions of the new materials in the field, and the reports of the activities of persons connected with the various places of English.

The English library, supported by the department, contains the latest fiction, biography, and travel books, which are available to the members.

DANCE CLUB

Dance Club was organized three years ago from a felt need that grew out of the Swing Out pageant a dance pantomime. Because a certain amount of program work is done yearly in dancing, Dance Club organized to be the study group for these programs.

To become a member you must have had previous work in dancing or have belonged to a dance class either at Indiana or elsewhere. To retain your membership you must own a dance work suit and maintain a high attendance requirement. Study meetings are held weekly. From three to four programs are presented yearly.

Officers for 1936-1937:
President .... Alberta Zerbe
Vice President . Anna Marie Roland
Secretary .... Dorothy Taggart
Treasurer .... Roberta Caldwell
Accompanist .... Alberta Zerbe
Sponsor .... Mazel Bowles

FRATERNITIES

HONORARY FRATERNITIES

KAPPA DELTA PI

ΚΔΠ

Membership in Kappa Delta Pi, an international honor society in education, is the highest academic honor that may come to a student at Indiana. Approximately twenty students are selected each year from the members of the Junior and Senior classes who have achieved better than a "B" average. Other criteria of selection are professional attitude, ethical standards, scholarship in the Department of Education, and consistency of "B" work.

Kappa Delta Pi is an educational society which selects from all departments of the college. There are one hundred and eight chapters in the leading colleges and universities The local chapter, Beta Gamma, carries on a very active program throughout the school year.

Freshmen should realize that competition is very keen for membership in Kappa Delta Pi and that the record for the first year is highly important.

Officers for the year 1936-1937 are:
President .... Trevor Hadley
Vice President .... Anne Davis
Rec Secretary Eleanor Jane Hunter
Cor Secretary   Elsie Garlow
Treasurer .... Ruth Sperry
Historian .... Dorothy Patterson
Counselor ..... Dr. Richard Madden

GAMMA RHO TAU

ΓΡΤ

Gamma Rho Tau is a national honorary and professional business education fraternity for men. Its purpose is to promote high scholarship and character, to encourage a research spirit, to advance the professional attitude of the teacher and to forward democratic ideals in education.

The qualifications for membership are good moral character, high scholarship, and promise of marked ability as a teacher of commercial subjects. Men in the Junior and Senior classes in the Department of Business Education who have these qualifications are eligible upon invitation to join the fraternity.

It should be the ambition of every man enrolled in the Department of Business Education to become eligible for election during his third year.

Beta Chapter has been functioning on the campus for eight years.

PI OMEGA PI

ΠΩΠ

Pi Omega Pi is a national honorary and professional business education fraternity for men and women in business education. The purpose of the fraternity is to encourage

high scholarship and high ethical
standards in business and professional life, and to emphasize service as
the basis of all worthy enterprise.
Junior and Senior students in the Department of Business Education who
have attained certain required standards in scholarship, character, and
professional attitude are eligible,
upon invitation, to join the fraternity.

Officers for the year 1937-1938 are:

President .... Frances Doyle
Vice President .... Sara Hess
Secretary .... Geraldine Tweed
Treasurer .... Robert Wiley
Historian .... Kenneth Nolan
Reporter .... Mae Armstrong

ALPHA PHI GAMMA

Α Φ Γ

Alpha Phi Gamma is a National
Honorary Journalistic Fraternity
which was founded at the Ohio
Northern University December 11,
1919. The purpose of this fraternity is to recognize individual achievement and ability in journalistic pur-
suits in college and universities, to
serve and promote the welfare of
the college through journalism, to
establish cordial relationships between the students and members of
the profession, and to unite in a
fraternal way congenial students interested in journalism,

Sigma chapter was established at Indiana 1928. Membership is open only to those who have served on the staffs of the college publications and have, in addition, a high scholastic standing.

Officers for the year 1937-1938 are:
President .... Harper Claycomb
1st Vice President ... Angie Holman
2nd Vice President .. Nina Rummel
Bailiff .... Sarah Winger
Secretary .... Jean Bryson
Treasurer .... Stephen Gendich

ALPHA OMEGA GEOGRAPHERS

Alpha Omego Geographers was organized as an honorary geography organization in 1928 by Miss Erna Grassmuck. The purposes of the organization are: to assemble geographic material, to discuss geographical themes, to promote fellowship and interest in geographic education, and to establish contacts with other groups in the field of geography by means of a national organization.

Requirements for membership are: declaration as a geography major, an average of "B" or better in at least four geography courses, acceptance by the group, and presentation of a satisfactory piece of original work. Both winter and summer students who are majors in geography are eligible.

Officers for the year 1935-1936:
President .... Leonard Pearson
Vice President .... George Getty
Secretary .... Florence Iiames
Treasurer .... John Becosky
Sponsor .... Mr. L. C. Davis

WOMEN'S FRATERNITIES

PANHELLENIC ASSOCIATION

The Panhellenic Association consists of representative's from the seven National Education sororities on our campus: Alpha Sigma Alpha; Sigma, Sigma, Sigma; Delta Sigma Epsilon; Alpha Sigma Tau; Pi Kappa Sigma; Theta Sigma Upsilon and Pi Delta Theta.

The object of this association is to furnish a forum for discussion of local inter-sorority affairs and to regulate all matters pertaining to sorority relationships, to establish standards of excellence in every line of sorority endeavor.

The Panhellenic offices are held in rotation .by sororities according to the time of their establishment on our campus; the advisors to Panhellenic are named in the same way.

Early in the fall Panhellenic sponsors a delightful tea for all Freshmen girls. In December we sponsor an inter-sorority dance. "Rushing" season opens for Freshmen in the second semester.

The officers for the year 1937-1938 are:

President ...... Mary Jane Snyder, Theta Sigma Upsilon
Rec. Secretary .... Betty Marlin, Delta Sigma Epsilon
Cor. Secretary .... Jean Bryson Alpha Sigma Alpha
Treasurer .... Juanita Barley, Pi Delta Theta
Advisor .... Laura M. Remsburg Pi Kappa Sigma

ALPHA SIGMA ALPHA

ΑΣΑ

Alpha Sigma Alpha is a professional-educational sorority that restricts membership to students in a degree curriculum. Including the local chapter, there are twenty-seven other sister organizations in colleges and universities throughout the United States. Alpha Gamma chapter was reinstated on this campus in March 1928.

With an open motto of "Aspire, Seek, and Attain," Alpha Sigma Alpha's ideals are to foster ambitions and ideals, and that richness of character and personality which will contribute most beneficiently toward the four-fold development of the physical, intellectual, social, and spiritual life of its members; to foster excellent scholarship and professionalism; to establish enduring friendships; and to maintain friendly contact and cooperation between not only chapter members but also with other campus organizations and the entire student body.

Alpha Sigma Alpha has an approximate membership of thirty. Throughout the year there are regular business meetings, on the social calendar there are dates for professional meetings, rush parties, the Mother-Patroness Dinner, Founder's Day Banquet, and the pledge party usually held in the Activities House.

Miss Ethel Belden is the faculty

advisor and Miss Joy Mahachek, the faculty sponsor. The patronesses are Mrs. George Simpson, Mrs. Harry Neal, Mrs. F. B. Stevenson, and Miss Florence Wallace.

The officers for the year 1937-1938 are:

President .... Arlene Miller
Vice-President .... Claire Cressman
Secretary .... Ruth Cox
Treasurer .... Rheva Miller
Registrar .... Lillian Porter
Chaplain .... Margaret Messner
Editor .... Helen Mellott
Collegiate Representative
                    Jean Bryson
Panhellenic Representatives
      Dorothy Hoey, Blanche Stufft

SIGMA SIGMA SIGMA

Sigma Sigma Sigma is one of the oldest national sororities. There are thirty chapters in other colleges and universities. It is a professional-education sorority, and its meetings each week are of that description.

Womanly character of the highest type, excellent scholarship, friendly cooperation with others, and social development are among the ideals of the sorority.

Lambda's social calendar includes a rush party, an annual pledge-professional dinner, Founders' Day Banquet, and many informal teas and parties.

The faculty advisor is Miss Edna Lee Sprowls.

The patroness list is as follows: Mrs. James Mack, Mrs. David Blair, Mrs. Harry White, Mrs. Allen Kirkpatrick, Jr., Mrs. Vernon Taylor, Mrs. John Keith, Mrs. Henry Tatnall Brown, and Mrs. Robert Sutton.

Officers for the year 1937-1938 are:

President .... Jean Davis
Vice-President ...... Sara Robeson
Rec. Secretary ...... Betty Kanable
Corr. Secretary ...... Betty Javens
Sentinel .... Barbara Turner
Keeper of Grades .... Fae Paul

DELTA SIGMA EPSILON

Δ Σ Ε

Of the seven national sororities at Indiana State Teachers College, Beta Chapter of Delta Sigma Epsilon is one of the oldest on the campus. For a period of several years, it, like the rest of the sororities, was absent during war times, but was reestablished in 1928. Usually known as the "Delts," the members consist of eighteen or twenty, yearly. There are thirty chapters in various colleges all over the United States.

The social calendar of Beta's is one of definite variety consisting of professional meetings, business meetings, social meetings, breakfasts at Rustic Lodge, rush parties, teas, hikes and a formal dance in the Spring.

Miss Lillian McLean is the capable sponsor of Delta Sigma Epsilon and Mrs. Edward Bennett, Mrs. Ernest Stewart, Mrs. Wallace Thomas, Mrs. Robert Fisher, Mrs. Blair Thomas and Mrs. Dale Timberlake are the patronesses.

The officers for the years of 1937 and 1938 are:

President
        Marion Upton, Vieva Wonder
Vice President ... Carriedna Bartley
Rec. Secretary .... Betty Marlin
Corr. Secretary ...... Mary Mabius
Treasurer .... Lucille Robertson
Sergeant-at-arms Rita Rose Monnich
Historian .... Virginia Davis
Chaplain .... Virginia Minnich
Keeper-of-Archives
        Carriedna Bartley
Panhellenic Representative
        Betty Marlin
Alternate .... Margaret Smith

ALPHA SIGMA TAU

ΑΣΤ

The Delta Chapter of Alpha Sigma Tau, national educational sorority, was installed at Indiana on May 27, 1916. During the war the sorority disbanded, but was reinstated on March 28, 1928. The aims of the sorority are to develop high standards of scholarship, true womanliness, and lasting friendships. The open motto of Alpha Sigma Tau is "Affection, Sincerety, Truth." The jewel is the pearl, the flower the yellow rose, and the colors emerald and gold.

Alpha Sigma Tau has fourteen active chapters in various colleges throughout the country and contains a strong alumnae of sixteen chapters. Delta Chapter has an active list of twenty seven girls sponsored by Miss Mary St. Clair King. Meetings are held weekly and sorority life is made complete through the various social functions which are held during the year.

The city patronesses of the sorority include Miss Marguerite Coe, Mrs. Harry Bartley, Mrs. Thomas Pealor, Mrs. Elmer Ellis, and Mrs. Alexander Stewart. The faculty members are Mrs. Karl Gasslander, Miss Dorothy Hoyle, and Mrs. M. J. Walsh.

The officers for 1937-38 are:

President .... Marion Weaver
Vice President .... Jean Colls
Rec. Secretary .. Margaret McFeeley
Treasurer .... Geraldine Tweed
Corr. Secretary.... Alice Ellenberger
Historian .... Marguerite Yates
Chaplain .... Jean Moore
Custodian .... Helen Garey
Panhellanic Representatives
Mary Ruth Fairchild, Jane Gillespie

PI KAPPA SIGMA

Π Κ Σ

Zeta chapter of Pi Kappa Sigma is one of the seven National Education sororities on the campus.

Pi Kappa Sigma has as its open motto, "In fun and in earnest." It's purpose is to cooperate with college authorities, to grow intellectually, socially, and morally and to realize that unity of sororities in the teachers field means mutual protection and improvement.

The "Pi Kaps" have approximately 30 active members. In addition to our regular meetings we have various types of parties, our annual Founders Day Banquet and several professional meetings during the year.

The Faculty adviser is Miss Laura M. Remsburg. The Patronesses are: Mrs. Hart Daugherty, Mrs. McClelland Gordon, Mrs. C. V. McCreight, and Mrs. R. N. Maloney.

Officers for the year 1937-1938:
President .... Hester Munden
Vice President ... Josephine Wesner
Rec. Secretary ..... Virginia Cassel
Corr. Secretary .... Clara Anderson
Corr. Editor ...... Dorothy Maurer
Treasurer .... Grace Eisaman
Keeper of Archives Georgia Ripple
Sergeant-at-Arms
                Mary Belle Campbell
Press Agent ...... Janet Stephenson
Panhellenic
    Josephine Wesner, Wilburta Jones

PI DELTA THETA

Π Δ Θ

Iota Chapter of Pi Delta Theta, a national educational sorority, was installed at Indiana in May 1935. It has at present twenty-seven active members.

Pi Delta Theta has as its open motto "Fellowship." Its purpose is threefold: (1) to foster close friendships, (2) to stimulate the social, intellectual and spiritual life of the membership and (3) to count as a force in the world through service rendered to others.

The faculty advisor is Dr. Reba N. Perkins. The patronesses include Mrs. Bruce Kendig, Mrs. Guy Kanable, Mrs. Harry Canfield and Mrs. C. E. Stede.

The sorority planned an interesting social life for its membership, including Founders Day, Fellowship Day, Christmas party and a Mother's Day Tea as well as a rush party. Pi Delta Theta sponsors a series of professional programs, varied in type.

The officers for 1937-1938 are:
President .... Vera Lauffer
Vice President .. Minerva Bechtold
2nd Vice President Irma Johnston
Secretary .... Eleanor Hess
Treasurer .... Alberta Kunsman
Registrar .... Geraldine Atkins
Chaplain .... Mardella Finch
Editor .... Virginia Sutherland
Panhellenic Representative
Juaniata Barley

THETA SIGMA UPSILON

ΘΣΥ

Pi Chapter of Theta Sigma Upsilon is one of the seven professional sororities on the campus. There are seventeen active chapters in various colleges and universities throughout the United States. Pi has at present twenty-eight active members.

The open motto of Theta Sigma Upsilon is "The Higher Good." Its aims are: to establish and maintain in the Chapter the highest standards of conduct and scholarship; to make the Chapter a powerful force in the life of the college and community; and to produce women who shall be noted for their sagacity, simplicity, sincerity, stability, and sympathy.

"Theta Sig," as it is known on the campus, sponsors regular meetings, a series of professional meetings, and an interesting social life for its members. The social affairs include; informal teas, rush parties, formal dinners, Founders' Day, and other special programs.

Pi's sponsor is Miss Grace Houston and its patronesses include: Mrs. Lawrence Davis, Mrs. Robert L. Clark, Mrs. W. W. Taylor, and Mrs. D. R. Tomb.

Officers for the year 1937-38 are:
President .... Doris Updegrave
Vice President ... Mary Jane Foster
Rec. Secretary .. Charlotte Hawkins
Corr. Secretary ...... Francis Urey
Treasurer .... Jeanette Scott
Editor .... Eileen Brassfield

Sergeant-at-Arms .... Louise Brown
Panhellenic Representatives
    Mary Stepanchak, Mary Elizabeth
        Feitt

MEN'S FRATERNITIES

INTER-FRATERNITY COUNCIL

The Inter-Fraternity Council consists of representatives from each
of the three social-professional fraternities; Phi Alpha Zeta, Phi Sigma
Pi, and Sigma Tau Gamma. The
Dean of Men is chairman of the
group.

The Council makes rules pertaining to inter-fraternity relationships
and aims to promote a friendly spirit of cooperation among the fraternities.

The rushing season and rushing
rules are fixed by the council. A
freshman entering school in September is not eligible for pledging to a
fraternity until April 1, of the second semester. One entering in January is not eligible until November
1. In order to be either pledged or
initiated, or in order to retain active
membership after initiation, one
must have at least a "C" average in
scholarship and no failures. It is
illegal for any fraternity to solicit
members before the dates when the
prospective members are eligible for
pledging. It is also illegal for any
fraternity man, in soliciting new
members to criticize adversely any
other of the three fraternities.

PHI ALPHA ZETA

Φ A Z

Organized in 1908 as Phi Alpha Fraternity. In 1927 Indiana's oldest established fraternity was incorporated as a national, educational, social, and athletic fraternity taking the name of Phi Alpha Zeta.

Installed as Alpha Chapter in 1927 Phi Alpha Zeta has always held a prominent place in the national organization. Twice she has had national presidents, and at present has the National Treasurer. At the Ninth Annual Convocation held at Geneseo, N. Y., May 15, 16, 1936 Russell Owens was elected Grand Treasurer. The national convocation is to be held in Indiana in May of 1937.

Alpha chapter publishes annually its fraternity magazine, THE ALPHIAN, which gives a detailed account of leading events of the year, the professional meetings, rush parties, alumni reports and many more news items of especial interest to active members and alumni.

The activities sponsored by the fraternity are: pledge smokers, pig roast, informal initiation, formal banquet, Valentine Party, inter-fraternity dance and a private Spring Dance. Each semester the fraternity holds three professional meetings. Some faculty member is usually engaged to address the group on subject of particular interest to prospective teachers.

The purpose of Phi Alpha Zeta fraternity is to help its members develop a well-rounded personality by fostering high scholarship, promoting fraternalism, and encouraging athletic ability. Members of Alpha Chapter can be found engaging in every worthwhile activity on the campus.

The fraternity roster includes 16 honorary members, the latest of these being Attorney-General Charles J. Margiotti and Superintendent of Public Instruction, Lester K. Ade, and a very active alumni association of over 400 men. The present membership is 40 active members and 20 pledges.

Alpha chapter of Phi Alpha Zeta maintains a comfortable fraternity house at 240 S. Eleventh St. Freshmen are always cordially invited to visit.

Officers for the year 1936-1937 are:

President .... Trevor Hadley
Vice President ... Robert Cronauer
Cor. Secretary ...... Joseph Henry
Rec. Secretary .. Ross Leslie Munn
Treasurer .... Richard Seifert
Chaplain .... Ward Gittings
Historian .... Harl Blose
Sergeant-at-Arms .. Frank Astorina
House Manager ... Wayne Halferty
Representatives to Inter-Fraternity
    Council .... Edward Lauther
Sponsor .... Mr. Tobias Chew

PHI SIGMA PI

Φ Σ Π

Phi Sigma Pi is a national professional education fraternity for men in teacher training institutions who have completed one year of college work, are enrolled in one of the degree curricula, and have a scholarship rating. Eta Chapter was installed at Indiana, April 30, 1929, and took the place of Omega Chi Fraternity, a local fraternity which had been active on the campus since 190^9.

Phi Sigma Pi is the only fraternity on the campus which is a member of the National Professional Inter-Fraternity Council which is made up of the foremost American Professional Fraternities. It is also recognized in Baird's Manual, Banta's Greek Exchange, and Phi Delta Kappa Directory.

Phi Sigma Pi is founded on the basis of superior scholarship and with the avowed purpose of advancing educational ideals. It is social in that it meets the need of close fellowship and social intercourse among men of interests in education.

Members of Eta Chapter are to be found in any worthwhile college activity. It is exceptionally well represented in the varsity athletic teams of the school, together with such other activities as dramatics, publications, honorary fraternities and professional clubs.

Membership in the fraternity this year exceeds forty men, most of whom live in the new fraternity house at 413 College Avenue, just off East Campus.

Each year the chapter holds at least six professional meetings. The fraternity is addressed by a faculty member or a guest speaker on some educational subject.

The "Lampadion," the official organ of the National Council is published three times a year. Eta Chapter publishes a chapter magazine, Eta News, in which appear the professional and social activities of the chapter. It makes its twice a year.

Each year the fraternity holds a Founder's Day Banquet at which time a leading educator is admitted into the fraternity as an honorary member. Eta's honorary members have been Dr. Keith, Dr. Graham, Dr. Rohrbach, and Ex-Governor Fisher. The last four Superintendents of Public Instruction have been members of Phi Sigma Pi. Twenty-seven college presidents are listed among its members. Some of the outstanding educators who belong are:

Dr. Ben Graham, Superintendent of Pittsburgh Schools.

Dr. Ballou, Superintendent of the Washington, D. C. Schools.

Dr. Q. A. Rohrbach, President of Kutztown State Teachers College.

Dr. Lee, Superintendent of Missouri Schools.

Dr. Reeder, Administration School of Ohio State University.

Officers for the year 1937-1938 are:

President .... Floyd Smith
Rec. Secretary ..... Kenneth Nolan
Corr. Secretary ..... John G. Cober
Sergeant-at-Arms ... Jack Stormer
Treasurer .... Albert Zanzuccki
Historian .... Paul Campbell
Chaplain .... Kennard Gaston
Representative Inter-fraternity
    Council .... Harper Claycomb

SIGMA TAU GAMMA

ΣΤΓ

Sigma Tau Gamma, the oldest national, social and educational and professionl fraternity operating exclusively in the State Teachers Colleges is represented on the Indiana campus by Pi Chapter. Alpha Chapter was founded at Central Missouri State Teachers College, Warrensburg, Missouri, June 28, 1920. Since then the organization has grown to include seventeen active chapters located in eleven different states.

Pi chapter was installed at Indiana November 8, 1930, taking the place of Phi Kappa Delta, a local fraternity. The following fall the chapter purchased their present home, a buff brick building, located just off East Campus at 257 College Avenue.

Requirements for membership to Sigma Tau Gamma include a high scholastic standing, excellent character, and a professional attitude. Fraternity activities include professional meetings, pledge smokers, pledging and initiation services, Senior Day Banquet and Inter-Fraternity Dance.

At the Senior's Day Banquet, held in the Spring, an Honor Man is selected. This person represents the ideal Sigma Tau Gamma Fraternity man concerning character, activity, both scholastic and social and interest in the Fraternity.

Through the influence of D. Kenneth Winebrenner, National Grand President, the National organization awards a standard Honor Key for excellence in scholarship and for leadership in activities. Brother Winebrenner is a member of the local chapter, having served as president of Pi Chapter in 1931. He was graduated in 1932 from the Art Department.

Officers for the year 1936-1937 are:

President .... Robert Hensel
Vice President .... Robert Allen
Secretary .... Clarke Hess
Corr. Secretary .... Kemit Palomaki
Treasurer .... Edward Breit
Historian .... Pearl David Lott
Chaplain .... Clarence Brown
Sergeant-at-arms .... John Davis
Sponsor .... Mr. R. S. Rowland

College

ship to
a high
char-
attitude.
profes-
smokers,
s. Sen-
Fratern-

t, held
Man is
nts the
Fraternity
activity,
and inter-

D. Ken-
Grand
nization
Key for
and for
Brother
of the lo-
as presi-
He was
Art De-

are
Hensel
Allen
Hess
Palomaki
Breit
David Lott
Brown
hn Davis
S. Rowland

ATHLETICS

GEORGE P MILLER

Coach

PRESCRIBED PHYSICAL EDUCATION

"Education for leisure and the enrichment of adult life is a fundamental problem affecting the welfare of the state and its perpetuity." Indiana State Teachers College believes this and provides equipment, facilities, and an instructional staff for carrying out a varied and comprehensive program of intramural athletics for men and women and varsity athletics for men.

The reorganized curriculum combines instruction in healthful living with physical activity. This new program begins this fall.

The prescribed program gives the student the kind of education through the physical that will enable him to meet the requirements insisted upon by superintendents of schools.

In addition to the prescribed program, every student (except during the practice teaching semester) will be given opportunity to participate in activities of their own choosing. These activities will be as varied as personnel and facilities permit. The student is required to participate in at least one activity each semester.

Some of the activities:

Fall	Winter	Spring
Archery	Basketball	Archery
Golf	Fencing	Golf
Hockey	Officiating	Life Saving
Swimming	Swimming	Scouting
Tennis	Volleyball	Softball

VARSITY ATHLETICS

Varsity athletics at Indiana are a definite part of the educational program. Athletics richly supplement and broaden modern education through development of virile men in manly activities. Our teaching profession is enriched by the calibre of men and that are fortified with the training and experience that varsity sports afford.

Football in the fall, forms the rallying point around which a real college spirit grows. School loyalty and enthusiasm gives the freshmen at the start of his career something in common with his upper classmen.

The public judges the tone of our school through our display of courage, skill and sportsmanship on the playing fields. We are proud of our record up to the present and anticipate further improvement with your help.

We are very anxious to have as many boys as possible participate in one or more of the following sports that go to make up our varsity program at the present time: Football, basketball, baseball, tennis, swimming and cross country.

FOOTBALL SCHEDULE

Sept. 25   Clarion, Home
Oct.   2   Lock Haven, Away
Oct.   9   Bloomsburg, Away
Oct. 16   Edinboro, Home
Oct. 23   Slippery Rock, Home
Oct. 30   Mansfield, Away
Nov.   6   California, Away
Nov. 13   Shippensburg, Home

BASKETBALL SCHEDULE 1938

Sat.	Jan.	8	
Tues.	Jan.	11	St. Vincent, Home
Fri.	Jan.	14	
Sat.	Jan.	15	California, Home
Tues.	Jan.	18	Clarion, Away
Fri.	Jan.	21	
Sat.	Jan.	22	Lock Haven, Away
Tues.	Jan.	25	Slippery R'k, Home
Fri.	Jan.	28	
Sat.	Jan.	29	Edinboro, Away
Tues.	Feb.	1	Lock Haven, Home
Fri.	Feb.	4	Frostburg, Away
Sat.	Feb.	5	California, Away
Tues.	Feb.	8	
Fri.	Feb.	11	Mansfield, Home
Sat.	Feb.	12	Bloomsburg, Home
Tues.	Feb.	15	Slippery R'k, Away
Fri.	Feb.	18	
Sat.	Feb.	19	Clarion, Home
Tues.	Feb.	22	St. Vincent, Away
Fri.	Feb.	25	Edinboro, Home
Sat	Feb.	26	
Fri.	Mar.	4	Shippensb'g, Away
Sat.	Mar.	5	Millersville, Away

MAY DAY CELEBRATION

This year the May Day activities did honor to our athletes. The athletic awards for the entire year were presented at an Assembly. Then came the All College Play Day on West Campus. This event affords opportunity for all students to engage in play. The event is never planed for weeks in advance. It is a spontaneous expression of the joy in physical activity. A swimming party, baseball game, and tennis match provide wholesome entertainment in the afternoon. The Athletic Dance in Recreation Hall puts final touches on a busy joyous occasion. This year our May Day took the place of the Athletic Dinner, the All College Banquet which for the past seven years has done honor to our athletes.

GIRLS ATHLETICS

Every girl who registers at Indiana automatically becomes a member of the Women's Athletic Association. Many activity groups which include mushball, archery, swimming, tennis, volley-ball, golf, scouting, hiking, fencing, field hockey and direct officiating, are open for enrollment for class credit in physical education, to earn points for the athletic awards, or for the mere enjoyment one may derive in the participation. The organization has as its aims the promotion of interest and efficiency in various sports as well as the fostering of physical recreation and fellowship.

The Women's Athletic Council, which includes the elected officers, the appointed managers of the various sports, and advisors from the physical education faculty, is the governing body of the organization. The Council has adopted a new plan for the awarding of the awards and will put it into effect beginning September 1937. For a grade of "A" in a sport in which the girl has enrolled for the awards, she will be credited with 100 points; for a grade of "B" she will receive 90 points; for a grade of "C" she will receive 80 points. For the first two hundred points acquired she will receive numerals; for each two hundred points beyond that she will receive a chevron. A total of one thousand (1000) points and a display of the characteristics which are necessary for excellent sportsmanship in all activities will entitle the girl to the award of the Varsity "I".

At the quarterly parties of the group, chevrons and numerals are awarded; the varsity "I" is awarded at the May Day assembly.

At several times throughout the year, Indiana is a guest at the Play Day of various colleges. At least once each year, Indiana is host to girls of other colleges for a playday.

Officers for the 1937-1938
Manager .... Agnes Burkhart
Assistant Manager Evelyn Buchheit
Social Chairman ... Vieva Wonders
Point Secretary ...... Dixie Beachy
Publicity Manager ..... Jean Davis
Secretary .... Dorothy Robbins

INTRAMURAL SPORTS PROGRAM

Since all students at Indiana are preparing for the Teaching Profession it necessarily follows that the aims of Intramurals as set forth at many colleges and universities which, in effect, are summed up in the phrase "Athletics for All," would not suffice. Briefly stated the aims of the Intramural Program for men at Indiana are:

1. To prepare students to organize and promote intramural or interclass sports in the Public Schools.

2. To teach students, who are not particularly athletically inclined, the

fundamentals and rules of sports which would fit into the intramural programs of the elementary and secondary schools.

3. To teach and train students in athletic activities in which they could indulge, in after-school life as a profitable use of leisure time.

4. An aid in developing personality and better feeling and understanding among the participants.

5. Athletics for present enjoyment and improvement of health.

The organization of Intramurals at Indiana consists of a Director, a Board of Control, and the Student Managers and Organizers, besides the participants themselves.

The Director of Intramural Sports is, Paul H. Boyts, a member of the Geography Department.

The Board of Control is composed

1. E. M. Sanders, Head Dept. of Physical Educ. Chair.

2. Paul H. Boyts, Director of Intramural Sports.

3. E. E. Prugh, Tennis Coach, and Asst. Basketball and Football Coach.

4 Geo. P. Miller, Director of Athletics and Head Coach.

5. Evan Williams, Intramural Manager.

Merit in Intramurals is recognized at Indiana by a service award given at the end of the Junior year to those men who meet the following requirements:

Merit in Intramurals shall be recognized by (1) An Honor Award, (2) An Efficiency Award.

The HONOR AWARD shall be a red, wool jacket with the Intramural Honor Award emblem attached on the upper, left front of the jacket.

The EFFICIENCY AWARD shall be the Intramural Efficiency Award emblem.

Requirements for the Efficiency Award:

1. The minimum participation each year for three years shall be:

a. One major sport and two minor sports, or

b. Two major sports ,or

c. Three minor sports

** Major sports: Tennis, Speedball, Volleyball, Basketball, Wrestling, Mushball, Handball, Swimming, Touch Football, Soccer, Track, Boxing.

Minor sports: Horseshoes, Cross Country, Foul Shooting, Ping Pong.

2. The participant must complete four different sports during his period of participation.

3. He must serve satisfactorily as a sports manager or as an assistant manager for a major sport, or as an organization manager.

4. He must earn 50 points by passing examinations on the rules and general knowledge of the game for various sports.

5. He must present a minimum of 250 points, of which not more than 100 shall be earned in a single year, exclusive of points earned under requirement No. 4.

Requirements for the Honor award.

1. At the end of each year, the three Junior participants who rank highest in points, and have not received a varsity letter in two or more sports shall receive the honor award. These students must have met all requirements for the Efficiency Award.

YELLS
Pep Yell

You've got it, now keep it,
Doggone it, don't lose it
    Your Pep—Your Pep.
You've got it, now keep it,
Doggone it, don't lose it
    Your Pep—Your Pep.
You've got it, now keep it,
Doggone it, don't lose it
    Your P—E—P.

Rah Yell

rrrrrRah — In-Di-An-A — rrrrrRah

Divided Team Yell

T E .... A M
T E .... A M
T E .... A .M
    Team, Team, Team

Individual's Yell

Yea (Coach)   Yea (Miller)
    Yea Coach Miller ! !

Alleganic—Ganic—Ganac

Alleganic—ganic—ganac
Alleganic—ganic—ganac
Hoo—rah   Hoo—rah
IN——DI——ANNN——A
I-N-D-I-A-N-A (spell)
INDIANA (yell)

Locomotive "I" Yell

I-N-D-I-A-N-A (slow)
I-N-D-I-A-N-A (faster)
I-N-D-I-A-N-A (fast)

SONGS

Alma Mater

To our noble Alma Mater's name
We, her chi.dren, sing a joyful lay,
And to her a new allegiance pledge,
That lives beyond a day.

REFRAIN

Sing, O. sing! Our Alma Mater's
praise,
Hail, O, hail! her color's gleaming
hue!
Give to her our homage and her love
And to her Name be true.

A prayer for her who sheltered us,
A hope no child her name will stain,
A cheer thrice giv'n with hearty
voice,
And now the sweet refrain.

Of Loyalty are symbols twain,
Her colors, crimson and the gray,
"Dear Indiana Mother Fair,"
The burden of our lay.

Words and music by
Mrs. Hamlin E. Cogswell.

SPIRIT OF INDIANA

On! On! On- On to victory,
  Everyone expects to see you win
    today.
Fight to win! "Play the game
    square!"
  Always for your Alma Mater do
    and dare!
Now then go! Give then not a show.
  You have skill and daring, that we
    know.
For not only will you score, but will
    add a few points more.
  Just to show them how we do at
    Indiana.

Indiana, don't you hear our cheer?
  That you'll honor us we have no
    fear.
See your pennant floating oe'r the
    field!
  Unto foeman you will never yield.
You will hear us as we shout and
    sing,
Other teams will know their fate,
  When they meet the "Red and
    Slate."
It's the way we always do at Indi-
    ana.

Victory! Victory! Victory!
  With your faces ever towards the
    foe.
Victory! Victory! Victory!
  Pressing forward down the field
    you go!
Victory! Victory! Victory!
  Every man is finding every play,

For 'tis written on your shield, .
  "Unto foeman never yield."
We will always do our best for Indi-
  ana.
      Words—Mrs. Hamlin E. Cogswell
      Music—Mr. Hamlin E.. Cogswell

The Beacon Light

In the ages long departed
  Slowly grew the need of light;
Beacons now illume each highroad
  Showing ways of Truth and Right.
Years ago our Indiana
  Raised her tower to the sky
Here a glowing beacon lifted
  Kindling hearts to purpose high.

CHORUS

Then it's hail to Indiana!
  From the East to boundless West.
Never burned a beacon brighter,
  Never was a way more blest
For the far off goal of learning;
  We who seek and catch her beam,
Send it forth to darkened byways
  In an ever-widening stream.

Our forefathers found the trail here
  Blazed where red men softly trod,
Patiently subdued the forest,
  Plowed and sowed the virgin sod;
And at last from labors lessened
  Looked they upward for the light,
Flaming from the beacon tower
  Where our College crowns the
    height.

      Words—Margaret Hawkins.
      Music—Carolyn Gessler.

Pennsylvania

Pennsylvania, my native state,
To you we pledge our devotion.
Pennsylvania, our loyalty is bound-
    less as the ocean.

REFRAIN

Pennsylvania, Pennsylvania, strong
    and true.
Pennsylvania, Pennsylvania, hear
    our song to you.
There is beauty in your mountains,
There is peace upon your hills,
And where e're I roam.
My only home is Pennsylvania.

Pennsylvania, we thrill with pride
To be your loyal descendants.
Pennsylvania, all hail to you,
The foundation of Independence.

School Song

Come and join our song of triumph,
Bring to Indiana's fame
Laurels of each new endeavor
That will glorify her name.
Forward then for Indiana!
Make these hills and valleys ring,
Lift her crimson and her silver gray
Honor to your Alma Mater bring.
Come, ye sons and daughters of her
    heart.
Each to his own valiant part,
Fight till you've won.
Then, the strife of battle done.
Sing, sing on for Indiana!

—Evelyn Jones.

CHURCH DIRECTORY

First Regular Baptist Church
S. W. Corner of Church Street and
Oakland Ave.
Rev. J. W. Kennedy. Pastor

St. Bernard's Catholic Church
N. W. Corner of Fifth and Oak Sts.
Father J. Brady
Father W. T. Mullen

Christian Church
S. W. Corner of Water and Fifth Sts.
Rev. R. B. Hurt, Pastor

Christ Episcopal Church
S. W. Corner of Ninth and Phila. Sts.
The Rev. Clement Gifford Belcher,
Priest in Charge

Evangelical Church
S. E. Corner of Fourth and Church
Rev. J. O. Bishop, Pastor

Zion Lutheran Church
S. W. Corner of Sixth and Church
Rev. A. J. Pfohl, Pastor

First Methodist Episcopal Church
N. W. Corner of Seventh and Church
Rev. Holt Hughes, D. D., Pastor

Wesleyan Methodist Church
N .W. Corner of Twelfth and Church
Rev. D. Rose, Pastor

First Presbyterian Church
S. E. Corner of Seventh and Church
Rev. Harry Burton Boyd,
D. D., LL. D.

First United Presbyterian Church
Church Street
Rev. Stillman A. Foster, D. D.

INDEX

CPSIA information can be obtained
at www.ICGtesting.com
Printed in the USA
BVHW081911231118
533818BV00005B/170/P

9 780260 445285